ANXIETY: A VERY VITAL EMOTION

Dr.Eden Payam Fazel
MD,MSc,Dip Coaching

For all brilliant minds
of the history
of mankind who were
accused of madness
by the mediocre majority,
and were detained,
tortured and humiliated
because of ignorance
and intolerance of others.

About Eden and "Survive and thrive"

Eden initially trained as a medical doctor specialising in preventive medicine and public mental health and later qualified as an individual and organisational Coach. Having worked in 31 countries across Africa, Asia, Europe and the Middle East as a medical trainer, organisational coach, and aid worker, he constantly remained curious to learn from every culture, lifestyle and tradition.

Eden soon realised that conventional medicine doesn't have the answers to all problems and that we need to resort to the nature within us and the nature without to survive and thrive.

Having been through various stretching life challenges, Eden survived and thrived, now sharing his experience with others.

He carried out extensive research into the natural behaviour of man and animals, to find out who we are, where we come from and what is the natural life style, that suits us best.

Eden is based in Hebden Bridge and travels across the UK and Europe to deliver his workshops to groups and organisations.

ANXIETY: A VERY VITAL EMOTION

Our emotions are our sixth sense, the vital powers that interpret, arrange, direct, and summarise the other five. Emotions tell us whether what we experience is threatening, hurtful, regretful, sad or delightful.

When emotions speak, we can only listen – and sometimes act – even if we don't always want to understand why.

Not to be aware of our emotions, not to appreciate, interpret and know how to express them is worse than being blind or paralysed. Not to feel is nothing less than death. More than anything else emotions make us human.

Emotions are the way we perceive ourselves. Emotions are our reaction to the world around us.
They are the way we sense being alive. When our emotions are settled we experience our highest consciousness.

Without emotions there is no existence, no life. Put simply, each of us is his emotions. What we feel about anything reflects our history and development, our past influences, our present turmoil and our future potential.

To understand our emotions is to understand our reaction to the world around us.

Anxiety is the fear of being hurt or of losing something. Whether the fear is real or imagined, it feels the same.

Fear, like all emotions, serves an important purpose – to

alert us to defend ourselves.
So when people try to pretend
they are not afraid, they
seldom do themselves any
good.

Fear protects us, and we
ignore it at our peril, whether
out of a desire to appear
strong or to evade the truth
of our emotions. When
fear warns us of danger,
it is summarising all the
information being received
by the five senses. Fear calls
our attention to a possible
threat to our well-being.

When you're exposed to a
threat, your body responds

by releasing powerful
stimulating hormones
into the bloodstream. These
hormones make the heart
beat more strongly and more
rapidly and also direct blood
flow to where it's needed most.
In a time of stress the blood
supply is usually diminished
to the abdomen and the
skin, and is increased to
the muscles. Most of the
physical symptoms of
anxiety – cold feet, butterflies
in the stomach, sweating,
dilation of the pupils of the
eyes and skin
pallor – are caused by these
hormones.

These stress hormones also make our minds "race", and increase our awareness of our surroundings.
An excess of this puts us constantly on guard, which in turn tends to immobilise.

What are most of us most anxious about? The answer generally is, losing our lives. Any psychology that doesn't consider the importance of the instinct to survive hasn't much to do with reality.
Few of us actually observe the instinct for self-preservation operating in real life, but we can detect or at least respond to it fairly readily in the

world of fantasy.
The feeling of taking a
risk and surviving is
invigorating. It gives a new
sense of life. That surely is
one reason why sports that
involve risk are so stirring.

In the real world anxiety
is common enough but the
potential aggressors in our
lives are seldom so clearly
defined. They're more likely
to be represented by the local
bureaucracy that asks us to
fill out a dozen meaningless
forms during an emergency,
wasting our time and
causing us needless stress;
or a government spending

our money irresponsibly
and threatening us
with jail if we don't pay
our taxes; or inflation
or recession and their
threat of unemployment.
We often feel helpless
confronting these threats.
The aggressor is simply too
powerful. Sometimes we
are not even sure where the
threat is coming from. The
government, the economy
are giant abstract threats,
threats without faces or an
approachable personality.

There is a time for defences
and a time for survival.
Fortunately, under great

stress, the decision is out of our hands. The lifting of defences becomes an instinctive act of survival. The mind is opened to seek out safety.

Most of us rarely feel threatened for our immediate physical survival. We have little sense of a real physical threat being overcome, and the enjoyment of relief that brings. Our modern age probably has deprived us of something by removing us from direct personal contact with the elements of nature. We find ourselves in an artificial arena, where our adversaries are arbitrary employers, demanding schedules, unfair practices and red tape – all of which create feelings of frustration and threaten us without giving us adequate opportunity for expressing our emotions about our condition.

We live in an unfair emotional bondage. We've been coerced into selling out our instinct for personal survival for something called "long term security," without being told beforehand of the consequences.

We never imagined that in our day-to-day living and working experience we'd be most threatened by our protectors. Worse, we seem to have few resources left to combat such threats, because to fight the system seems overwhelming.

If we were to examine the "system," we would see that the security it offers is elusive. It depends on the system working. When hard times come the system isn't working and the loyalty of the organisation toward its employees may be difficult to discern, and the situation

may produce more anxiety than security. The modern world is driving many of us crazy!

The answer is that each of us – to whatever extent possible – must take our survival back into our own hands. We may not do as well financially, but if we can lower the anxiety level by being more in control of our own destiny, we've come out ahead.

When it seems impossible to manage directly the stress of working for a corporation or contending with government bureaucracy, other outlets for resolving tension have got to be found. One such is a sport that offers physical and emotional challenge that can be met and overcome.

It's very rewarding to pit oneself against a mountain in winter and conquer the steepest slopes. You may not have beaten the boss, you certainly have not made the tax laws any more equitable, but you have overcome a real challenge, and you have demonstrated your ability to "make it." The system may no longer work, but you still do!

It's our modern civilisation itself that's at the root of a

great deal of our anxiety and stress. Industrialisation has often progressed at the expense of the individual. The exigencies of corporate and industrial life dictate that we suppress our instinct for survival and suffer in silence the anxieties such a life produces – a depleting experience, because to suppress any emotion requires energy.

To live in a world where some organisation professes to know what is best for us and expects us to go along blindly with its policies is putting the survival of that organisation above our own.

No company or organisation that places the survival of itself over the well-being of any single member can ever act in keeping with the real needs of the individual. We sense this and feel uncomfortable on the job, a little used, perhaps a little like an impersonal number.

Many businesses today are creating products on one end of the assembly line and dehumanised workers on the other. Working with faceless machines in which one's only interest is in keeping one's hands or clothing out of the gears is boring.

The usual way people defend themselves against such monotony is to block it out and retreat into the world within.

This turning away from the world only adds to the feeling of boredom. Anxiety and boredom tend to go hand in hand, and often result in such disorders as depression and alcoholism.

This sense of helplessness in a mechanised world gradually undermines our ability to take charge of our private lives.
We tend to erect such a

protective screen against our anxiety at work that when we return home those same screens stay with us.

When we look for the nurturing and love that we're missing on the job, we're often disappointed as we frequently make unrealistic demands on those we love to compensate us for our unhappiness. Often our stressful anxiety makes it difficult for us to see that those we turn to at home also have their own needs. As work stress increases so does the imperviousness of our defences, and the richness of our personal and family life diminishes.

Often we don't recognise what's really happening until the damage has already been done. We "reason" that the times aren't the best, that one should be thankful for bread on the table.

But what job is truly worth this kind of emotional suicide?

We can only react purposefully to a threat if we perceive it.

Few of us are so self-aware that are able to understand exactly what we fear, and therefore we are unable to relieve fully our feeling of anxiety. Some are even unaware that what they are feeling is anxiety.

How do you cope with these emotions? Before you can do anything about your anxiety, you must first be able to admit that you are anxious. This may not be as simple as it sounds.

Many people have peculiar notions about their emotions. They believe to admit feeling frightened is to admit being weak. They deny their anxiety and try to pretend nothing is wrong.

Whenever you deny your anxiety you only undermine your ability to defend yourself from whatever is threatening. To say that you are not anxious is the same as saying there's no threat.
How then do you explain your emotions? And what purpose do they serve?

When you feel anxious you are perceiving a threat, even though you may not be aware of it. Don't ignore anxiety. Anxiety means that something you consider important is being threatened.

The rest of us have had our senses so bombarded by our environment that we tend to block out the incoming stimuli that would alert us to what's threatening.

Each of us needs to raise his awareness of his own emotions and perceptions. If we try to block out what makes us anxious, what frightens us, we set ourselves up for greater suffering. Better to do something about problems when they're small and can most easily be coped with.
If we constantly block a threat from our awareness,

it consumes more and
more energy. As it grows
it eventually does break
through and overwhelm us.

When a defence stands
between you and your ability
to perceive your true emotions,
it also stands between you
and your best chance of
survival. To be anxious
is to feel uncomfortable.
It's supposed to feel
uncomfortable. If anxiety
weren't uncomfortable, people
wouldn't do anything to get
rid of it!

The feeling of anxiety is
best removed by removing

the threat that caused it, not by defensively denying or ignoring it.

If you're in danger you should know it. If you rely on someone else to act in your best interests when you're threatened, then something is very wrong in your life. To leave responsibility for your safety to another person or an institution may be helpful in quieting your fears for the moment, but eventually it undermines the natural process of self-survival.

Being anxious and afraid may tend to bring

back childish feelings of helplessness, but admitting you're afraid doesn't mean that you're a child.

When we feel afraid it is only natural to wish that someone "bigger," more capable and powerful, will come to our rescue.

Modern society sends us two conflicting messages:

1) be self-reliant, be yourself, take charge of your own destiny; and 2) conform, play the game, be a "good" citizen! Individuality is often labelled eccentricity,

tolerated in theory only; conformity is expected in practice.

Meeting our obligations to society and earning it's prescribed rewards too often may not fulfil our emotional needs. We want something more but don't know where to look. What we find is a sea of anxiety. Out of fear, we tend to follow a course chosen by others who claim to know the "right" direction. No wonder so many of us feel anxious so much of the time! We're beginning to lose our initiative, our sense of ourselves, of our own life's goal and purpose.

For many, these words may sound inconsistent with the hard cold practical facts of life. A person has to work, to get along or worry about being fired. Well, yes and no. That's the message we have been conditioned to accept. It isn't necessarily the reality of our best interest or even survival. It is the message of somebody else; of a structure that has its own self-interests, not necessarily the same or even consistent with the individual's in question.

The real fact is that many of us give up or give in too easily, without even looking for alternatives or testing them. We fear the uncertainty of newness. This does not mean that we should give up job, family and society for some mystical inner voice. But at least give your best self a chance.

Listen to yourself; accept your responsibility for solving the threats to your life and well-being, at least to the extent that you can from the resources within you. This at least is a start at being a free person. And isn't that what we're all supposed to be about?

Each of us feels vulnerable in a different way. If you know your vulnerability you know a great deal about yourself. As we've seen, everyone is vulnerable to the loss of a loved one, the loss of control, and the loss of self esteem.

Dependent people are especially vulnerable to loss of love, either because as children they experienced such a loss or because they lived with the threat of separation or rejection. They go through life feeling a loss, even before they have lost anything.

The next kind of loss that produces anxiety is the loss of control. Whether it's power, money, position, influence or title that we value most; few of us look as unhappy or as desperate as "controlling" people who feel they are about to lose control.

People who most fear losing control are those who make a special point of being in control all the time. They live by rules. They feel most comfortable when they know the precise limits of a given situation. They can relax only when they are sure they understand how everything fits. Even then they may be on the lookout for things that could go wrong and they invent extra routines to perform - to make certain that what hasn't gone wrong won't. When things do start to get out of control, they tend to get more and more involved in the rules and details of the system, and begin to regard them with an air of permanency or even religiousness. They imbue them with a ritualistic or magical quality in an effort to exorcise their anxiety. Consider a lady or gentleman who makes a revision of the shopping list by rows to correspond with the supermarket displays, who keeps the house pristine, who pays bills by return mail, whose cheque book balances to the penny, whose calendar is planned months ahead, thereby getting the unknown under control as well. Is this person really in control?

In fact for many controlling people, their order and routine seem more important than their emotions. Because the loss of control is so frightening, they tend to control the pieces of their world in increasingly minute details, making still

longer and more accurate lists, keeping a still neater house or office. They would do better to admit they feel hurt and anxious and to realise that this is what makes them feel out of control. When you experience a feeling without hiding it, it passes most quickly and drains you the least.

The loss of esteem also triggers anxiety. It may appear as a fear of failure, a fear of being exposed as worthless or a fear of being ridiculed. People who live in fear of being embarrassed often try to hide their real

emotions.
They may pretend that their
emotions are unimportant,
or that the test of their worth
didn't count.

Such people are often
competitive and unsure of
their worth at the same time.
They feel anxious not only
when they're put down, but
when other people exceed
them. They rarely act as
themselves, but in a way they
think will make them appear
worthwhile to others.They
rarely make an honest effort
to succeed, but just enough
to give the impression of
success. Ironically, the effort

needed to succeed is usually only a little more than that required to save face.

True success can't be achieved until you're willing to be judged on your performance. Not wanting to be so judged, a person overly concerned with esteem shies away from making a full effort in order to protect his fragile self-image. The person really isn't sure he or she could be first, and not knowing how well he or she could do, dreads ever finding out.

Now the question is: how do we go about managing anxiety?

Since anxiety is a warning, it's vital that we first understand what dangers we are being alerted to - the warning must be broken down into usable information. Sometimes it's awfully difficult to tell if the danger causing the alarm is in the present or in the past.

Managing anxiety primarily in the present is less difficult. When you feel anxious for reasons not clear to you or when a situation that should make you happy only makes you feel threatened, stop and think. The first step in getting control over anxious

situations is to ask yourself,
"What is it I'm so afraid
of losing?" Asking that
question sometimes gives
enough distance to begin
to solve the problem. The
question begins to define the
answer.

The office worker afraid to
ask for the raise, the tenant
afraid to arouse the ire of
his neighbour whose radio
blasts him deaf every night,
the boy afraid to ask the girl
for a date – and vice versa
in these changing times!
– All may feel generally
anxious without knowing
why until they begin to

stop and think and ask themselves the question "What am I afraid of losing?" And in reply may come, respectively, the answers: my job, a "friendship", my masculinity, my femininity.

Most people face some anxiety every day of their lives. Lawyers become anxious when they have to appear in court. Accountants become anxious before an audit. Professors become tense when they have to lecture. Students become worried before exams. Hostesses become jittery before a party. Directors

become distraught before
opening night.

Theirs is preparation anxiety.
It's the fear of being a flop,
of losing face. This anxiety,
in moderate amounts, helps
to get a person charged up
to do his best. It's common
to everyone who stands up
to be counted. But often the
level of anxiety associated
with performing is so high
that it keeps many even from
trying. Moderate so-called
stage fright, however, is not
a disease and only when it
actually prevents you from
working does it need to be
treated.

Chronic anxiety is difficult to manage and painful to endure. A person suffering from it feels constantly as if he were about to suffer a great loss. He uses up most of his energy trying to hold his anxiety in check.

As a result even small amounts of stress quickly overwhelm his ability to cope. As his defences become spread over too wide an area in an attempt to cover all possible threats his anxiety begins to leak out everywhere. Defences become useless. In fact, he becomes so caught up in the management of

his defences that he has little
energy left over to live.
Many people suffer from
anxiety without realising
it because their defences
against anxiety keep
them from being aware of
themselves. Our society
makes emotional cripples out
of many people who can't cope
with the lack of
clear cut goals and rewards
that have little real meaning.
We still need some space,
time, privacy and peace, if
only for a few minutes each
day.
We need an opportunity to
get in contact with ourselves,
to listen to our thoughts,

to pay attention to our emotions.

Even though it seems impossible at times, the best way to manage anxiety is to avoid unnecessarily threatening situations and to begin to make yourself the most complete and strongest person you can be. To do this you need to accept who you are, take responsibility for your life, and make certain that you are heading in the direction that is right for you. This is a difficult job. To be one's own person, you need not be entirely free of anxiety, but at least you can know what you fear and be

free to change what
threatens you.
A free person accepts
responsibility for both the
good and the bad in his
life. He is aware of his own
vulnerability and instead
of concealing it he uses it.
He allows himself to be open
to the pain of his world.
Through that special window
he can see more clearly,
because he feels more.

A free person doesn't waste
time and energy getting
involved in things that
can't be changed but instead
focuses on the areas he or she
can affect. He or she doesn't

let the world "get to him/her."
He or she simply defines what
his/her goals are and works
honestly and energetically
toward them.

One of the most important
goals of life is to become
familiar with yourself in a
positive way. To reach this
point requires acceptance
of your limitations. You
need to understand that no
matter how badly you may
have been treated or what
your personal circumstances
happen to be, no matter
how cruelly abandoned or
rejected you may have been
or where you are in life now,

you are always in charge of your own life – you have the primary responsibility to make good on your talents and abilities. Hopefully the disappointments and rejections you experience will someday be seen as a proving ground for you.

If you are a person who has been brought up in a dependent way, your outlook need not always be one of disappointment and hurt over losses. Your own special sensibilities about being dependent may allow you to become a person with extraordinary nurturing qualities that allow you to identify with and help people who haven't yet outgrown their dependent ties. Once a person has overcome his own dependency problems he becomes free to give, to support, to encourage and to sustain – to do everything that is the opposite of draining other people. The anxiety he felt in being afraid of dependent losses will gradually disappear as he begins to see himself as a person of strength.

In the same manner controlling people, once they learn to overcome their defensiveness, also have a great deal to give. They have a special understanding of loneliness and isolation. People who have learned to overcome their need to be in control all the time can be very helpful to others in showing them how to organise and reach toward a self-fulfilling goal.

And finally people who've been anxious about self-esteem can learn to be less self-centred and more concerned with the job they're doing than the impression they make on others. They can learn to respect what they do for sake of itself, rather than constantly worry about being worthy in the eyes of others.

So when weaknesses are converted into strengths, people are transformed from dependent, controlling or esteem-seeking members of society to nurturers, managers and performers, and each has a great deal to give and teach the others.

Although anxiety carries the threat of impending loss and injury, it doesn't obscure the very positive and real aspects of its other function – to alert and build up the self into its highest potential. We can do this by accepting the hurts that have come to each of us, having done with the pain, learning the lessons of our early experiences, and growing into the best person we can salvage from our past and create through the actions of our present.

Each of us is the architect of his own future, and if we use our best personal building materials we have nothing to fear. Merely being on the road to the discovery of one's best self lowers anxiety.
The rest is work and time.

Everyone moves at his own
pace and in his own way.
No one can create your life
for you. No one is supposed
to. A good doctor, coach,
psychologist, or teacher,
is only an instrument, a
catalyst, not more! Others
may point the way, help
define your goals, but
the work, the burden, the
responsibility – and therefore
the joy – are yours alone.

You see now, after all anxiety
is a very vital emotion.
You need to make friends
with it, listen to its message
and put it to good use.

Good luck

WORKSHOPS

Finding Your
Gift and Writing
your Action Plan

Are you living the
life that is right
for you?

SURVIVE AND THRIVE
WORKSHOPS

Keys to hardiness, resilience and coherence

Are you best fit to Survive and Thrive in the face of adversity?

SURVIVE AND THRIVE
WORKSHOPS

Negotiation & assertiveness in volatile Contexts

Learn to protest now not to become a doormat forever!

SURVIVE AND THRIVE
WORKSHOPS

DiY Counselling,
DiY Coaching

Why don't you do
it yourself?

Biophilia

Learning from natural man and animals: lessons from Ethology

SURVIVE AND THRIVE
WORKSHOPS

Anger a very
healthy emotion!

Making friends
with anger and
making it work
for you

WORKSHOPS

Taking good risks

The art of risking: assess, prepare, commit and complete good risks!

SURVIVE AND THRIVE
WORKSHOPS

Knowing your
blind spots

Explore your
strengths and
weaknesses

Please contact us through our
website to attend our workshops

Email: surviveandthrive@doctors.net.uk
Website: www.surviveandthrivecoach.org.uk